Chris Rice

The songs featured in this songbook are from the following recordings:

PAST THE EDGES
Cassette #080688588847, CD #080688588823

DEEP ENOUGH TO DREAM
Cassette #080688529741, CD #080688529727

Transcribed by **Brent Roberts**

Edited by **Bryce Inman**

The following Studio Series accompaniment tracks are available from these recordings:

TITLE	CATALOG NUMBER
And Your Praise Goes On	080689 657641
Big Enough	080689 655647
Deep Enough to Dream	080689 561642
Missin' You	080689 659645
Naive	080689 656644
Prone to Wander	080689 562540
Sometimes Love	080689 554347
Welcome to Our World	080689 548346
Wind and Spirit	080689 658648

in association with

rocketown records™

Chris Rice *past the edges*

When I imagine the size of the universe
And I wonder what's out PAST THE EDGES
Then I discover inside me a space as big
And believe that I'm meant to be filled up
With more than just questions

My three-and-a-half pound brain has long been intrigued by the enormity of the universe. Then, just when I'm almost overwhelmed by it, my thoughts turn to eternity and God, and my physical universe, with all its galaxies and light-years, suddenly shrinks and almost disappears in His shadow. My mind can't bear thoughts of that magnitude for very long, so I race back to my speck of a planet, and my unimpressive ability to take up about a square foot of its surface at any given moment, and marvel that these extremes of existence are curiously intertwined. My smallness somehow matters in the realm of God's hugeness. The moments of my life are somehow connected to forever. My steps are very small, but they are ordered by the very great Creator. Looking back over the past year, I see the evidence.

After twelve fruitful years of full-time teaching, singing and worship leading in youth and college retreat settings, I wondered how my life would change this year with the release of *Deep Enough to Dream* on Rocketown Records. I have no question that I am alive to be involved personally in the lives of students, and to use those friendships to encourage their faith and their pursuit of the heart of Jesus. I was concerned that releasing this record would interfere with this most important part of what I do: the relationships.

As I expressed this concern to my friends at Rocketown Records, their response, without hesitation, was their determination to support what I was already doing with my life, not to change it. They only desired to help make the music born in those relationships available to more people—people whom I would never have a chance to connect with personally.

None of us knew if this would work. The label was taking a risk with their first artist, a guy who wasn't going to be available most of the time for promotion. They carefully chose which industry events for me to be involved in without interfering with my ongoing retreat and camp schedule. Their choices seemed right. And looking back confirms that our steps are ordered by the Lord.

My calendar is still packed with camps and retreats, and my life is still filled with teenagers. In addition, I receive letters and e-mail daily from students and adults I've never met who are being affected by my life and work. Some have come from as far away as Thailand, Indonesia, Australia, New Zealand and Korea. The results have surprised us all—on both personal and professional levels.

I was in Maryland in February, leading a spiritual emphasis week at a high school, when Michael W. Smith tracked me down to pass on the news that I had received six Dove Award nominations. What an exciting time for a new label and a new artist! Well, I didn't receive any of the Doves, but I recall the next week doing a concert in Tulsa, OK, and leading the audience in a chant of "0 for 6"! I then received from them "The Parrot Award" (a colorful talking stuffed animal which they awarded me to make up for my Dove-lessness)! The year also brought several chances to perform with Michael at some of his concerts, a few festivals, television appearances on CeCe's Place, Prime Time Country, the E! channel's Talk Soup, and even appearances at Promise Keepers events.

I was blessed this year to do a song on *Exodus*, a praise and worship project featuring some of the artists I have come to admire for their work, some of whom have become my friends this year. I was also able to participate on a tribute record for Rich Mullins, singing "Calling Out Your Name," my favorite of his songs. This new adventure with Rocketown Records has taken me to places I would never have imagined. And all the while, I have been able to maintain the relationships with kids all over the country, and continue leading them through worship and friendship.

Now, we're launching into the second record, *Past the Edges*. Reading through the lyrics of these new songs, I notice a lot of questions being asked, and not always answered. These songs reflect my work over the past year with students. Students ask the greatest questions. Some are yet unanswerable. My desire is to help them run in the right direction with the questions. Even if we don't get answers, we can trust that God is big enough to hold all the answers for us until it is time for us to know them. That time may come in this lifetime, but it will more likely come when we are finally with Him.

The God who lives out past the edges of the universe, and out past the edges of our own understanding of fairness and holiness, has chosen to race across the boundaries from the corners of creation all the way to the deepest places in our tiny selves. To love us, to brave the questions, and to hold us when there are no answers yet. With *Past the Edges* I want to ask boldly, along with those who don't yet believe, and with those who believe. Because asking is moving, and the whole point of our existence is to move—to move toward the One who is so far away and so close at the same time.

Chris Rice

Printed by Davis Brothers Publishing Co., Inc., Waco, Texas

contents

Smellin' Coffee

**Words and Music by
CHRIS RICE**

Easy groove ♩ = 112

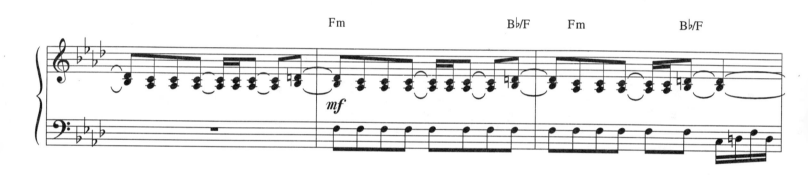

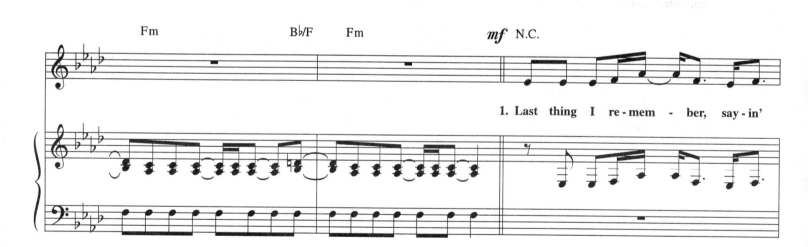

1. Last thing I re-mem-ber, say-in'

10

11

CODA

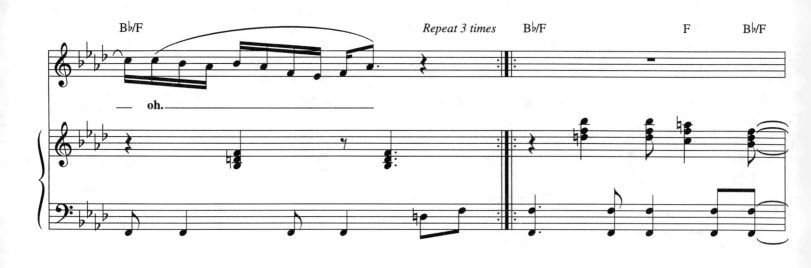

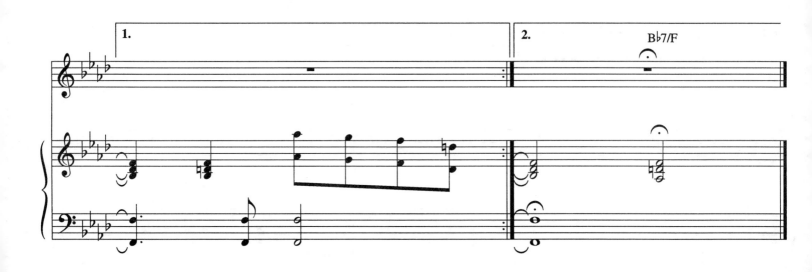

Naive

Words and Music by
CHRIS RICE

Easy four ♩ = 92

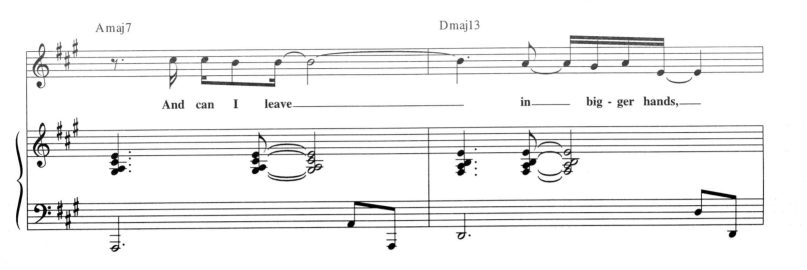

And can I leave_____ in_____ big - ger hands,_____

and may I be_____ so bold_____ to ask_____ You,_____ to ask_____

_____ You,_____ to ask_____ You_____ how_____ long?_____

The Power of a Moment

Words and Music by
CHRIS RICE

-ment,_____ yeah._____

Ooo._____

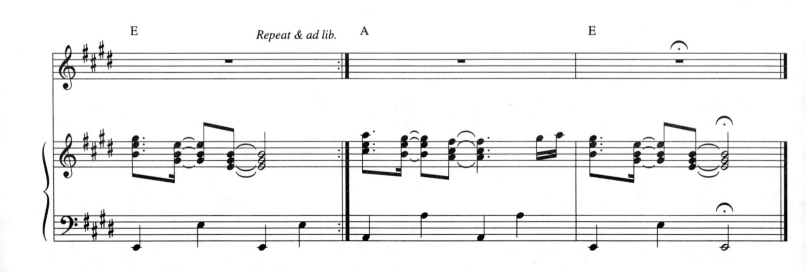

Big Enough

Words and Music by
CHRIS RICE

36

And Your Praise Goes On

Words and Music by
CHRIS RICE

Easy pop $\quad \bullet = 72$

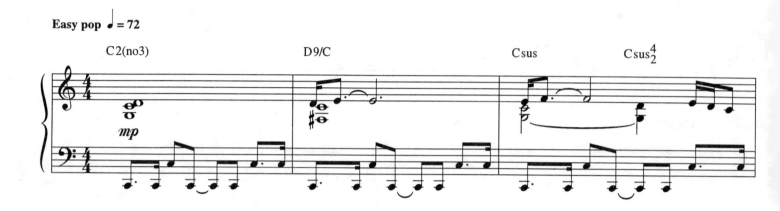

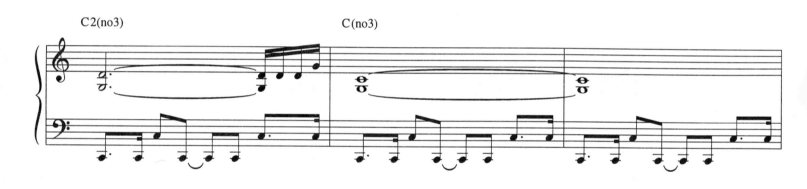

1. The moon is high___ and the sun - set fades,

the lull - a - bies____ have all____ been   sung.

We're tuck - ing in____   an - oth - er   day____

and stars ap - pear____ now one____ by   one.____

But the still - ness moves____ and the si -   lence   yields

praise goes on._____ I'll be run - ning___ to_____ Your___

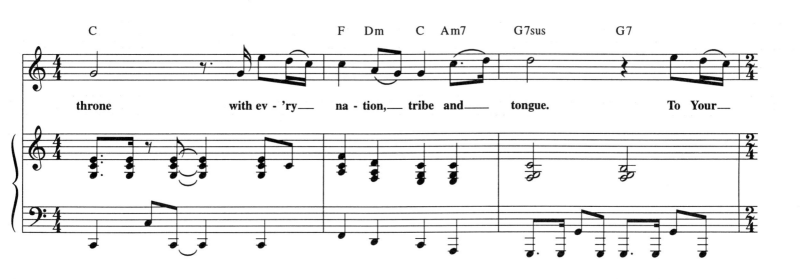

throne with ev - 'ry___ na - tion,___ tribe and___ tongue. To Your___

arms I'll fly,_____ I'll gaze in - to Your___

48

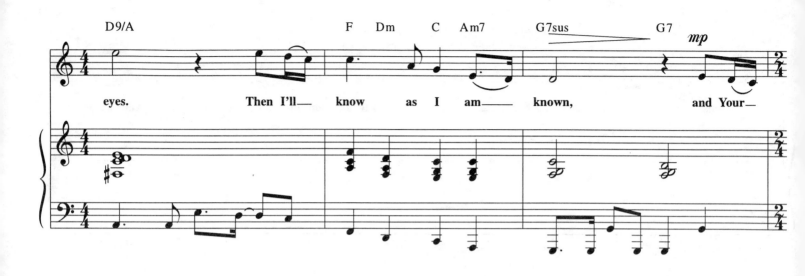

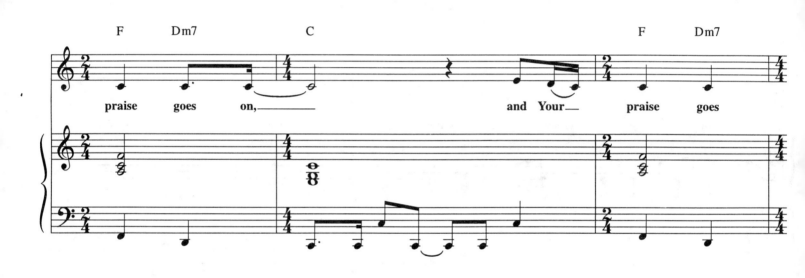

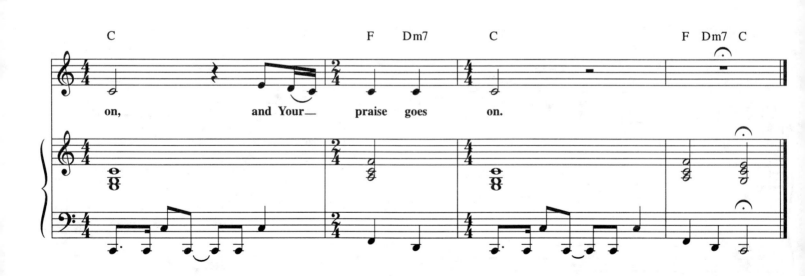

Live By Faith

**Words and Music by
CHRIS RICE and
SCOTT MacLEOD**

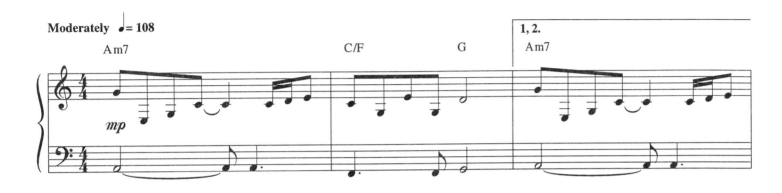

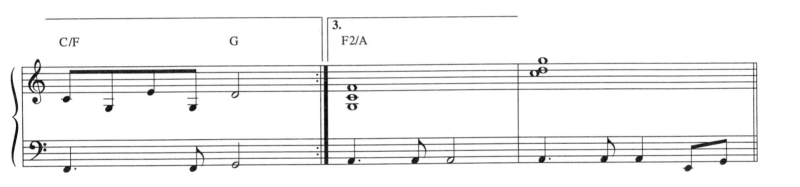

1. I can't feel You mov - in' in - side, I don't hear____ Your voice whis - per - in'____

52

to live___ by faith, got to live___ by faith

keep liv - in' by faith, keep liv - in' by faith.

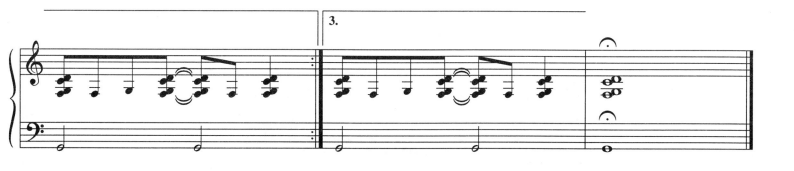

One of Those Days

Words and Music by
CHRIS RICE

Gentle acoustic pop ♩. = 66

1. Oh,_____ it's been__ one of those days_____ when you walk__

__ with me so____ close I think I caught the scent of____ an -

- gel wings. And my,____ oh__ my,____ un - sus - pect - ing heart

60

63

Wind and Spirit

Words and Music by
CHRIS RICE

Driving! ♩ = 112

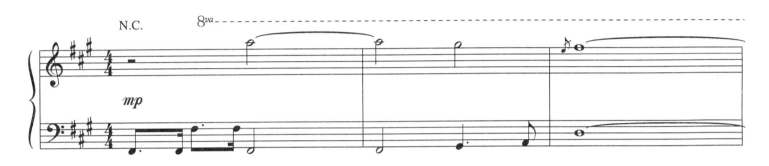

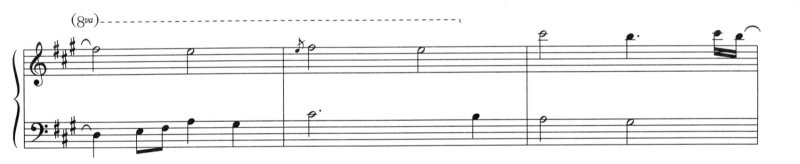

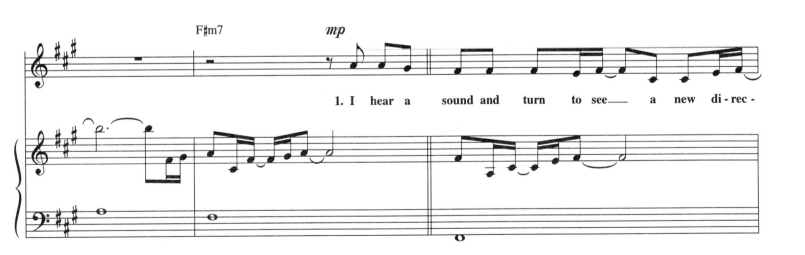

1. I hear a sound and turn to see___ a new di-rec-

68

-li-ness,_____ stir-ring my soul to___ ho -

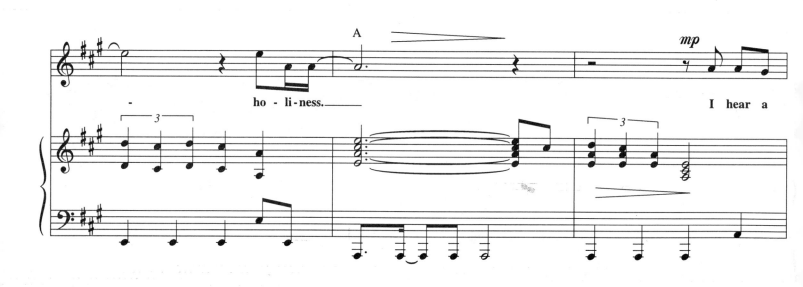

- ho - li-ness._____ I hear a

sound and turn to see___ a new di-rec - tion on___ that rust - y weath-er-vane.___

Thirsty

**Words and Music by
CHRIS RICE**

Gently ♩ = 76

1. I'm so thirst - y, I can feel it burn - in' through

the furth - est corn - ers of my soul. Deep de - si -

re, I can't de - scribe this name - less urge

78

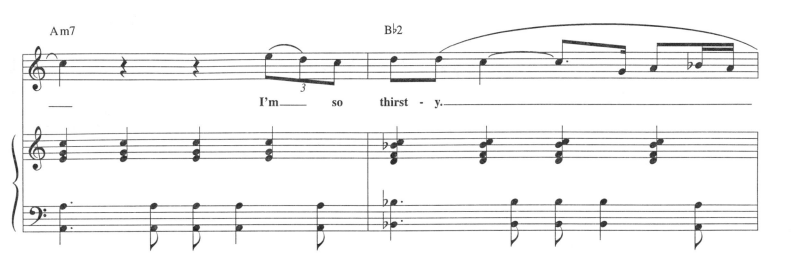

I'm____ so thirst - y.____

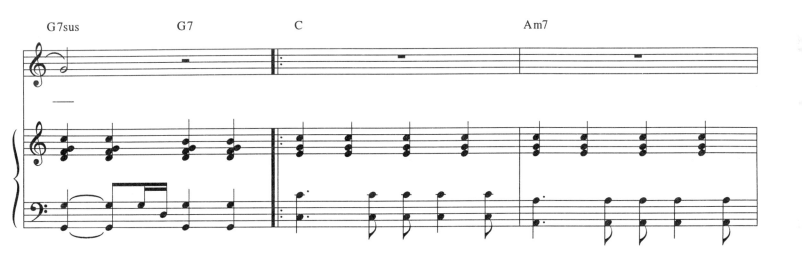

ad lib. on repeats

Missin' You

**Words and Music by
CHRIS RICE**

With emotion ♩ = 84

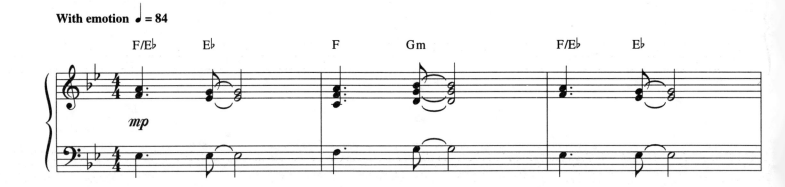

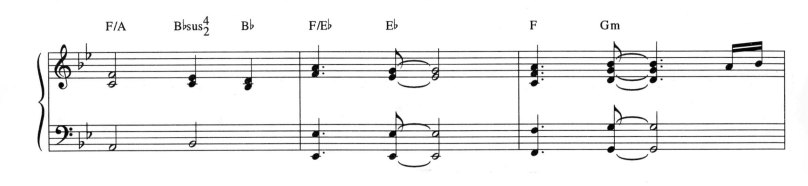

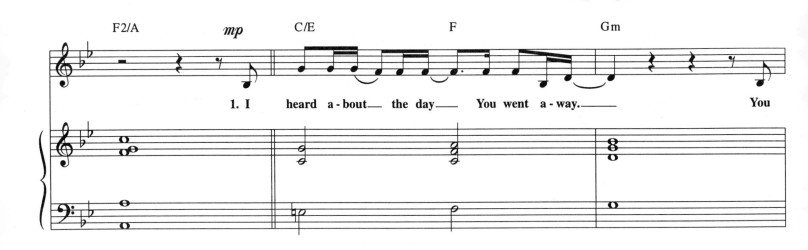

1. I heard a-bout the day You went a-way. You

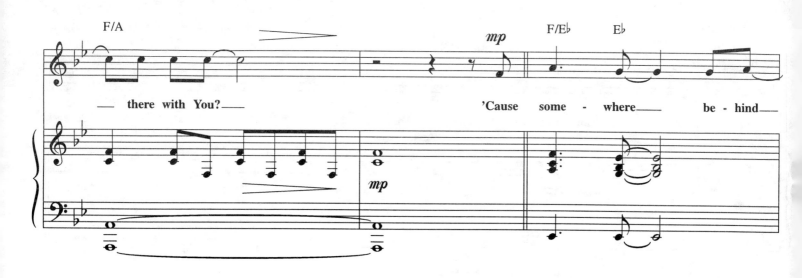

til I find___ the place___ You've made for me._____ But still I'm

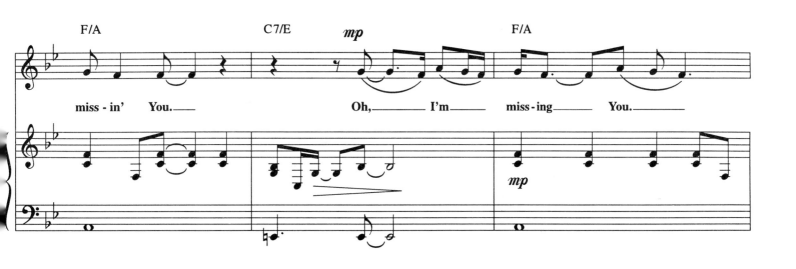

miss - in' You.___ Oh,___ I'm___ miss - ing___ You.___

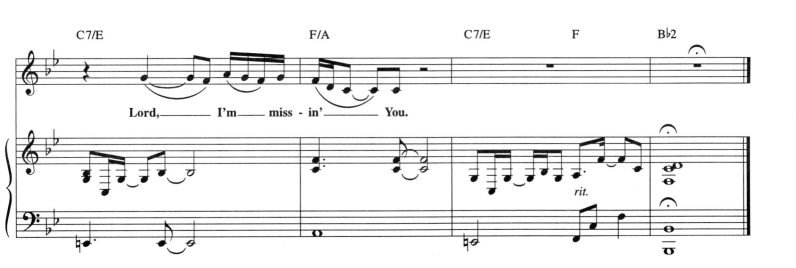

Lord,___ I'm___ miss - in'___ You.

Clumsy

Words and Music by
CHRIS RICE

94

Deep Enough to Dream

Words and Music by
CHRIS RICE

Acoustic pop ♩ = 96

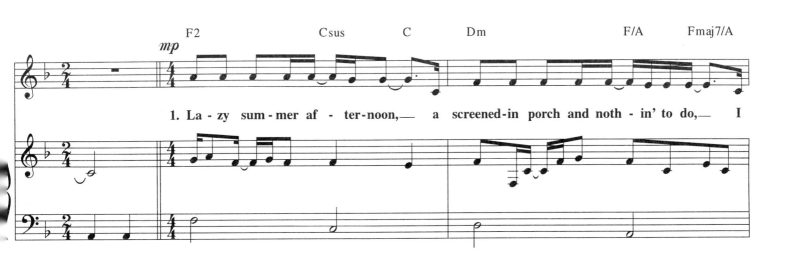

1. La - zy sum - mer af - ter-noon,—— a screened-in porch and noth - in' to do,—— I

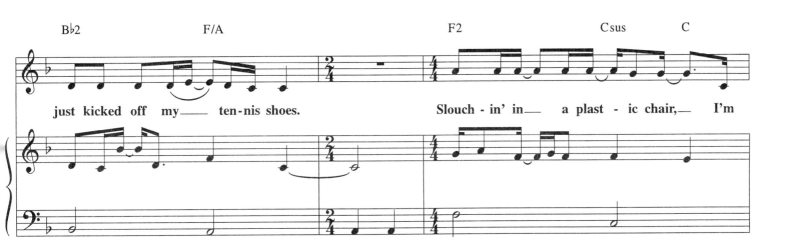

just kicked off my——— ten-nis shoes. Slouch - in' in——— a plast - ic chair,—— I'm

N/A

Hallelujahs

Words and Music by
CHRIS RICE

Worshipfully ♩ = 76

1. A pur - ple sky to close the

107

108

I Need a Hero

Words and Music by
CHRIS RICE

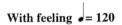

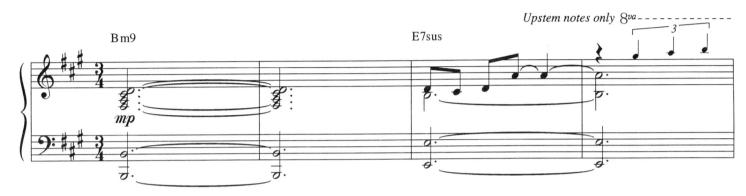

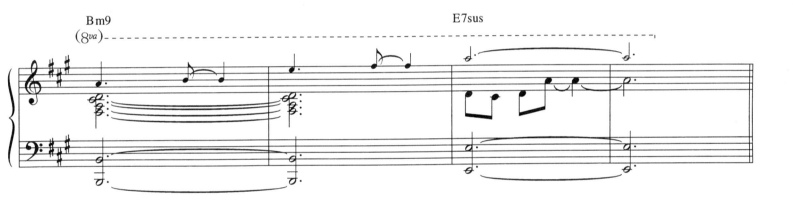

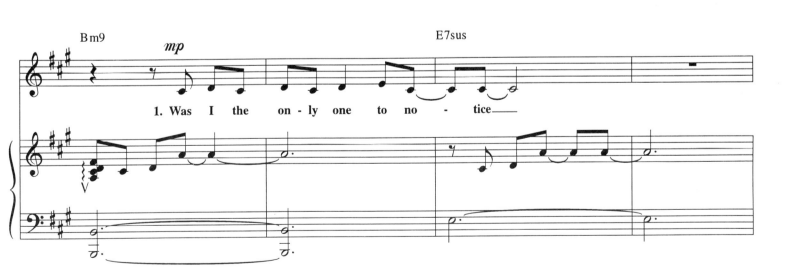

1. Was I the on-ly one to no - tice____

114

116

I need_____ a he -

Sometimes Love

Words and Music by
CHRIS RICE

123

own hand,____ in - to its_____ own hand.____

f *Guitar solo (ad lib. freely)*

Welcome to Our World

Words and Music by
CHRIS RICE

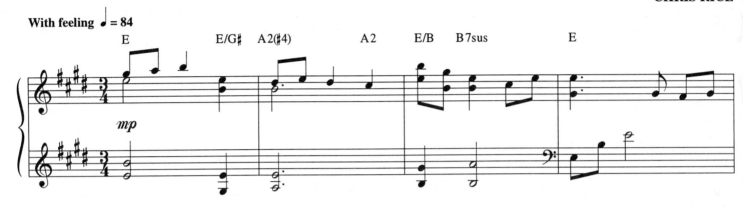

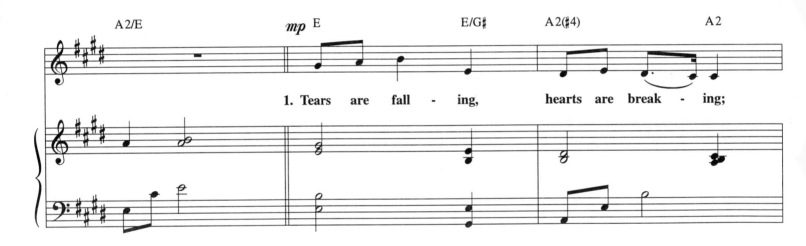